# "IT'S NOT JUST DARK IN SCANDINAVIA."

BO BRENNAN

# INSTA GRAMMAR
# NORDIC

LANNOO

@IRENEFINNE

@IRENEFINNE

@IRENEFINNE

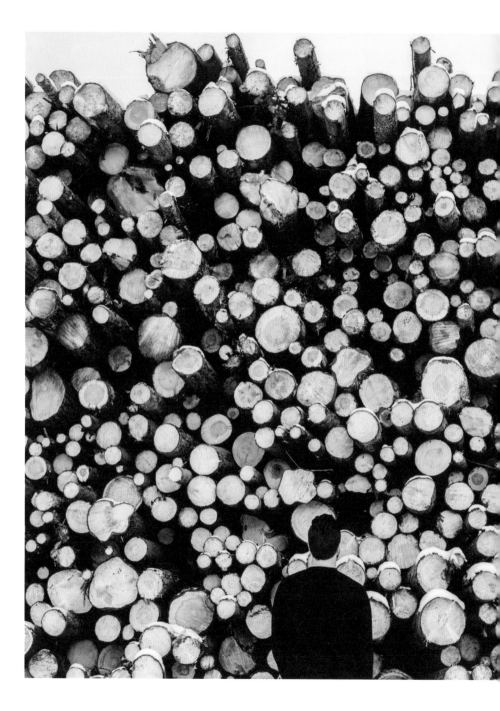

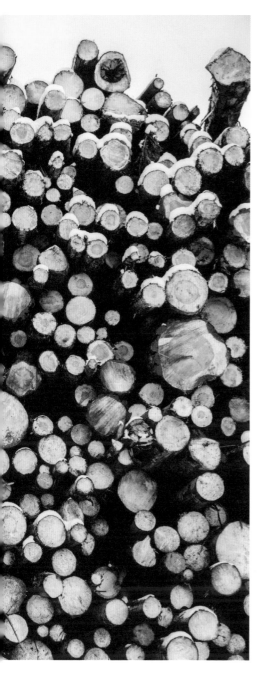

@FLICKANOCHTANTEN

# "THERE'S SOMETHING I LOVE ABOUT HOW STARK THE CONTRAST IS BETWEEN JANUARY AND JUNE IN SWEDEN."

BILL SKARSGÅRD

@MISAUNTE

@MISAUNTE

@SLAVASTE

@SLAVASTE

@SLAVASTE

# "ON EARTH THERE IS NO HEAVEN, BUT THERE ARE PIECES OF IT."

JULES RENARD

@SUNDAYS_AND_TEA

@TERHOM

@ANGELIQE.NU

@SUNDAYS_AND_TEA

@MEYERSMAD picture by @schonnemann

@MEYERSMAD picture by @schonnemann

@MEYERSMAD picture by @schonnemann

"EVEN THE
SMALLEST
OF STARS
SHINES IN THE
DARKNESS."

@NIKOLAJTHANING

@METTEDUEDAHL

@METTEDUEDAHL

@TERESE_K

@LEKESTOVE

@LEKESTOVE

# "WINTER WONDERLAND IS ON MY HAND, IT'S KINDA ROCKY"

NICKI MINAJ

# "DENMARK IS A SMALL PLACE

MADS MIKKELSEN

@LINETHITKLEIN

# WE ALL KNOW EACH OTHER."

@KRISTINENOR

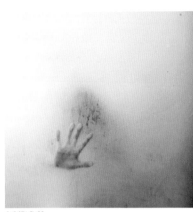

@KRISTINENOR

@KRISTINENOR

@KRISTINENOR

@KRISTINENOR

# "AUTUMN ARRIVES IN EARLY MORNING, BUT SPRING AT THE CLOSE OF A WINTER DAY."

ELIZABETH BOWEN

@ANNETTEPEHRSSON

@ANNETTEPEHRSSON

@ANNETTEPEHRSSON

@ANNETTEPEHRSSON

@ANNETTEPEHRSSON

@ANNETTEPEHRSSON

@ANNETTEPEHRSSON

@ANNETTEPEHRSSON

@ANNETTEPEHRSSON

www.lannoo.com
Register on our website for our newsletter with
new publications as well as exclusive offers.

Photo Selection/Book Design:
Irene Schampaert

Cover image:
@angeliqe.nu

Also available:
Insta Grammar Cats
Insta Grammar City

If you have any questions or remarks, please contact
our editorial team: redactiekunstenstijl@lannoo.com.

© Uitgeverij Lannoo nv, Tielt, 2016
D/2016/45/256 – NUR 652/653
ISBN 9789401436946